AF575327

UNEARTHING EARLY HUMAN REMAINS

REBECCA FELIX

An Imprint of Abdo Publishing
abdopublishing.com

abdopublishing.com

Published by Abdo Publishing, a division of ABDO, PO Box 398166, Minneapolis, Minnesota 55439.

Printed in the United States of America, North Mankato, Minnesota
052018
092018

Design: Sarah DeYoung, Mighty Media, Inc.
Production: Mighty Media, Inc.
Editor: Megan Borgert-Spaniol
Design elements: Mighty Media, Inc., Shutterstock, Spoon Graphics
Cover photographs: Alamy, Shutterstock, Spoon Graphics
Interior photographs: Alamy, pp. 8 (top, bottom), 13, 15; AP Images, pp. 19, 27; iStockphoto, p. 11; Shutterstock, pp. 4, 5 (all), 7, 9 (right), 17 (bottom left), 21 (right), 25, 29; Wikimedia Commons, pp. 9 (left), 17 (top, bottom right), 21 (left)

Library of Congress Control Number: 2017961585

Publisher's Cataloging-in-Publication Data
Names: Felix, Rebecca, author.
Title: Unearthing early human remains / by Rebecca Felix.
Description: Minneapolis, Minnesota : Abdo Publishing, 2019. | Series: Excavation exploration | Includes online resources and index.
Identifiers: ISBN 9781532115288 (lib.bdg.) | ISBN 9781532156007 (ebook)
Subjects: LCSH: Paleoanthropology--Juvenile literature. | Human remains (Archaeology)--Juvenile literature. | Discovery and exploration--Juvenile literature. | Excavations (Archaeology)--Juvenile literature.
Classification: DDC 599.938--dc23

CONTENTS

THE HILLS HAVE BONES

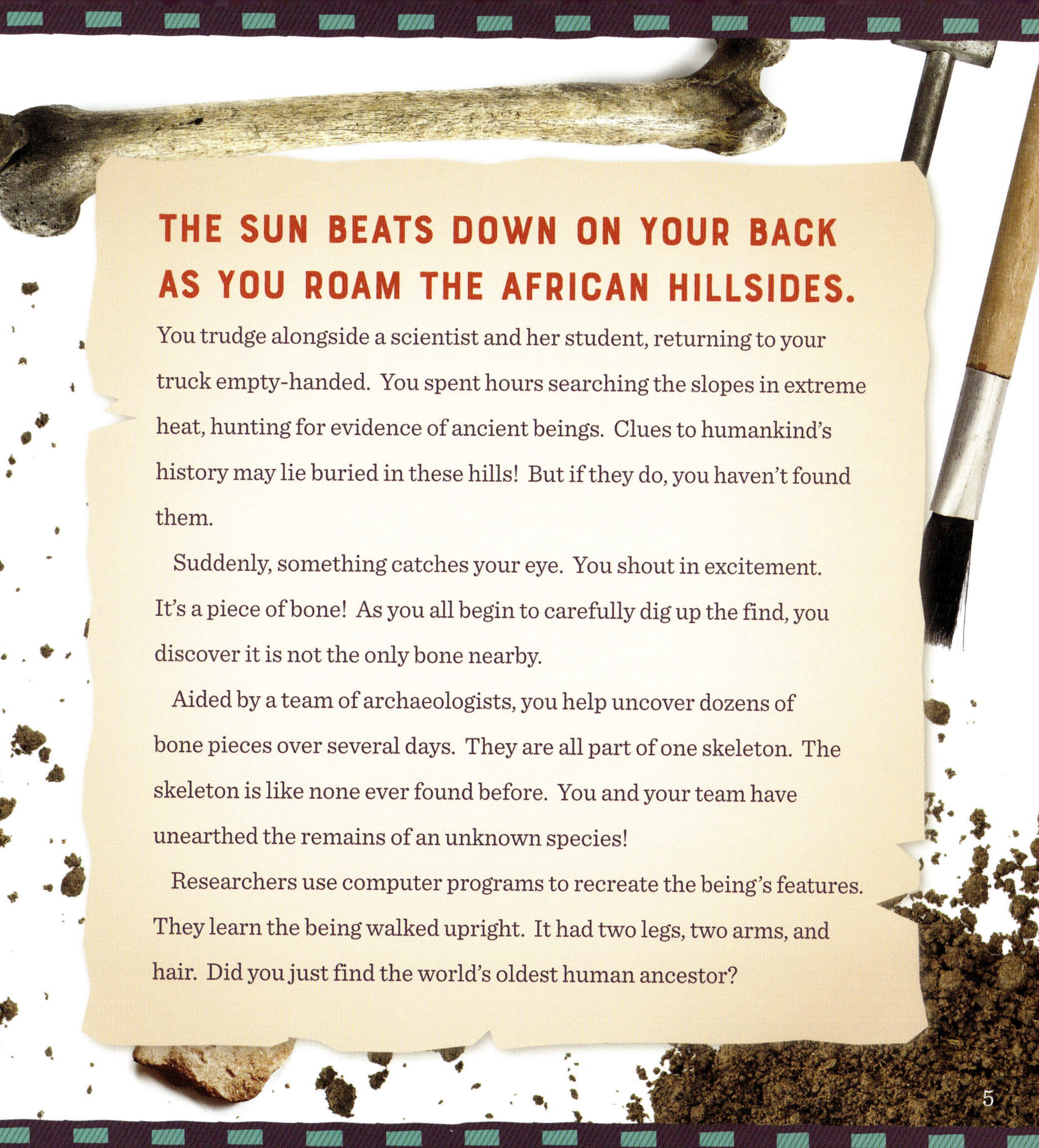

THE SUN BEATS DOWN ON YOUR BACK AS YOU ROAM THE AFRICAN HILLSIDES.

You trudge alongside a scientist and her student, returning to your truck empty-handed. You spent hours searching the slopes in extreme heat, hunting for evidence of ancient beings. Clues to humankind's history may lie buried in these hills! But if they do, you haven't found them.

Suddenly, something catches your eye. You shout in excitement. It's a piece of bone! As you all begin to carefully dig up the find, you discover it is not the only bone nearby.

Aided by a team of archaeologists, you help uncover dozens of bone pieces over several days. They are all part of one skeleton. The skeleton is like none ever found before. You and your team have unearthed the remains of an unknown species!

Researchers use computer programs to recreate the being's features. They learn the being walked upright. It had two legs, two arms, and hair. Did you just find the world's oldest human ancestor?

WHAT ARE EARLY HUMAN REMAINS?

Early human remains are body parts of past human-like species. These species are the early ancestors of modern humans. Archaeologists search for these remains to understand human origins.

Formal study of early human remains began about 150 years ago. Since then, scientists have found bones from about 6,000 ancient human-like individuals. These remains come from several species.

Neanderthals are one of the most famous human-like species. It was once thought that modern humans **evolved** directly from Neanderthals. But this is not the case. Most archaeologists now believe ancient humans and Neanderthals lived at the same time. The species are relatives that split from a common ancestor about 500,000 years ago.

However, this is relatively recent in the record of human-like fossils. Scientists have found human-like species that lived much earlier than Neanderthals. In fact, the oldest human-like remains ever found are as many as 7 million years old! These species help piece together the puzzle of human origins.

Paleontologists study the skull shapes of early humans and other primates to help determine the size of their brains. As early humans evolved into modern humans, their brain size increased.

TIMELINE

1859

Charles Darwin publishes his ideas about human **evolution.** This spurs the archaeological search for human origins.

1868

Ernst Haeckel writes about a "missing link" species between humans and orangutans.

1891

Eugène Dubois digs up "Java Man" in Indonesia. The human-like bones are later dated to 700,000 years old.

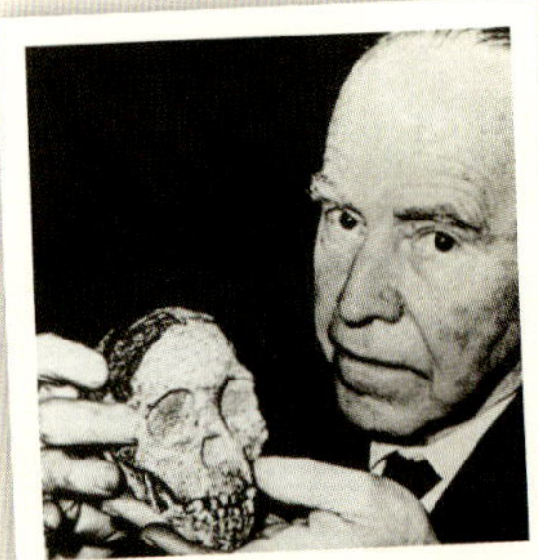

1924

Raymond Dart excavates "Taung Child" from rock in South Africa. It is dated to 2.8 million years old.

1994

Scientists discover the remains of a new human-like species in Ethiopia. Nicknamed "Ardi," the skeleton is 4.4 million years old.

2001

Michel Brunet finds "Toumai" in Chad. The human-like skull is dated to between 6 and 7 million years old.

1974

In Ethiopia, Donald C. Johanson unearths the bones of a 3.2-million-year-old skeleton later nicknamed "Lucy."

2017

Viviane Slon discovers **DNA** from ancient human-like species in sediment from around Europe and Asia.

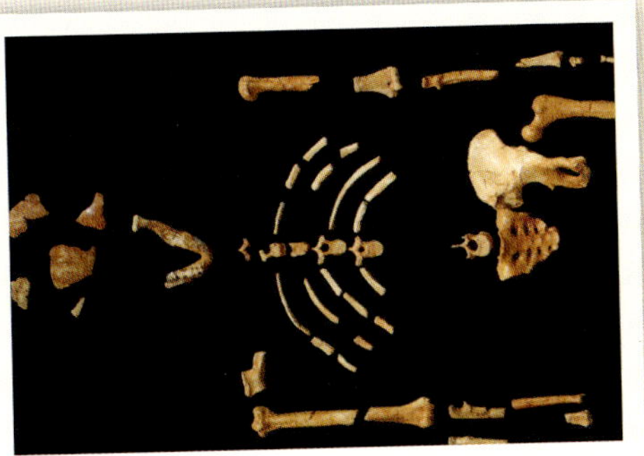

CREATION CONTROVERSY

The theory that humans and apes share a common ancestor is accepted as scientific fact worldwide. But it has also caused **controversy** throughout history. Since the beginning of time, humans have wondered how they came to exist. But ancient peoples did not have advanced knowledge of science. So, they turned to religion to explain their existence.

For centuries, the widespread belief was that a god or gods created humans. In 1859, British scientist Charles Darwin famously challenged this idea. He stated that modern species **evolved** from other species over millions of years. Changing species slowly developed new features to help adapt to their **environments** and survive. Through this process, they became new species.

According to Darwin, humans and apes shared an ancestor. This idea outraged religious organizations around the world. But Darwin's theory of evolution spread far and wide. It led many people to think critically about human origins. And, Darwin's

Charles Darwin presented his theory of evolution in his 1859 book, *On the Origin of Species*.

theory made sense to many archaeologists. They began searching for early human remains to tell the story of **evolution**.

SEARCHING FOR THE MISSING LINK

Proving human **evolution** fascinated researchers. In 1868, German scientist Ernst Haeckel presented his idea on the topic. He believed a **bipedal** species must have existed as the "missing link" between apes and humans.

Dutch scientist Eugène Dubois read about the missing link. He wanted to find fossils of it. So in August 1891, Dubois went to the Indonesian island of Java. He searched along the Solo River, where local farmers had found fossils.

In October, Dubois dug up a rounded bone. It was the top of a skull! The next year, Dubois found a femur, or thighbone, in the same pit. Its structure showed it was from a bipedal species. Dubois believed the femur and previously found skull represented the missing link between apes and humans. He published his findings.

Geologists studied Dubois's findings. These scientists could help archaeologists estimate the ages of rock containing fossils. Fossils would be the same age as the surrounding rock. Geologists dated the skull and femur, nicknamed "Java Man," to 700,000 years old!

But because this was an estimate, critics doubted Java Man's age. Archaeologists continued the hunt for even older remains. In 1924, Australian scientist Raymond Dart succeeded without even going on a dig.

Dubois gave Java Man the scientific name *Pithecanthropus erectus*. Scientists determined Java Man would have been about 5.6 feet (1.7 m) tall when walking upright.

Dart was living in South Africa. One day, a skull **embedded** in rock was delivered to his home. Miners had found it while digging in a lime **quarry** in the South African town of Taung.

After three months' work, Dart broke the skull free. It had a face with teeth. Some teeth were still breaking through the gums. This meant the skull was of a child. Geologists dated the skull to about 2.8 million years old!

Dart decided the skull, nicknamed "Taung Child," was human-like. He shared his findings. They supported Darwin's idea that early humans came from Africa, home to many ape species.

However, most scientists at this time believed early humans came from Europe or Asia. They said Taung Child was from an ape species. Others said an adult specimen of the species would better show what it was.

In 1936, Scottish paleontologist Robert Broom accomplished this. Broom

DIG THIS!

Eggshells and animal bones were buried in the same site as Taung Child. Because of this, scientists believe the child may have been prey to an eagle. Wounds under the skull's eye sockets, possibly from a sharp beak, support this theory.

Raymond Dart was a professor of anatomy when he received the skull of Taung Child. He determined the skull was larger than an ape's but smaller than a human's.

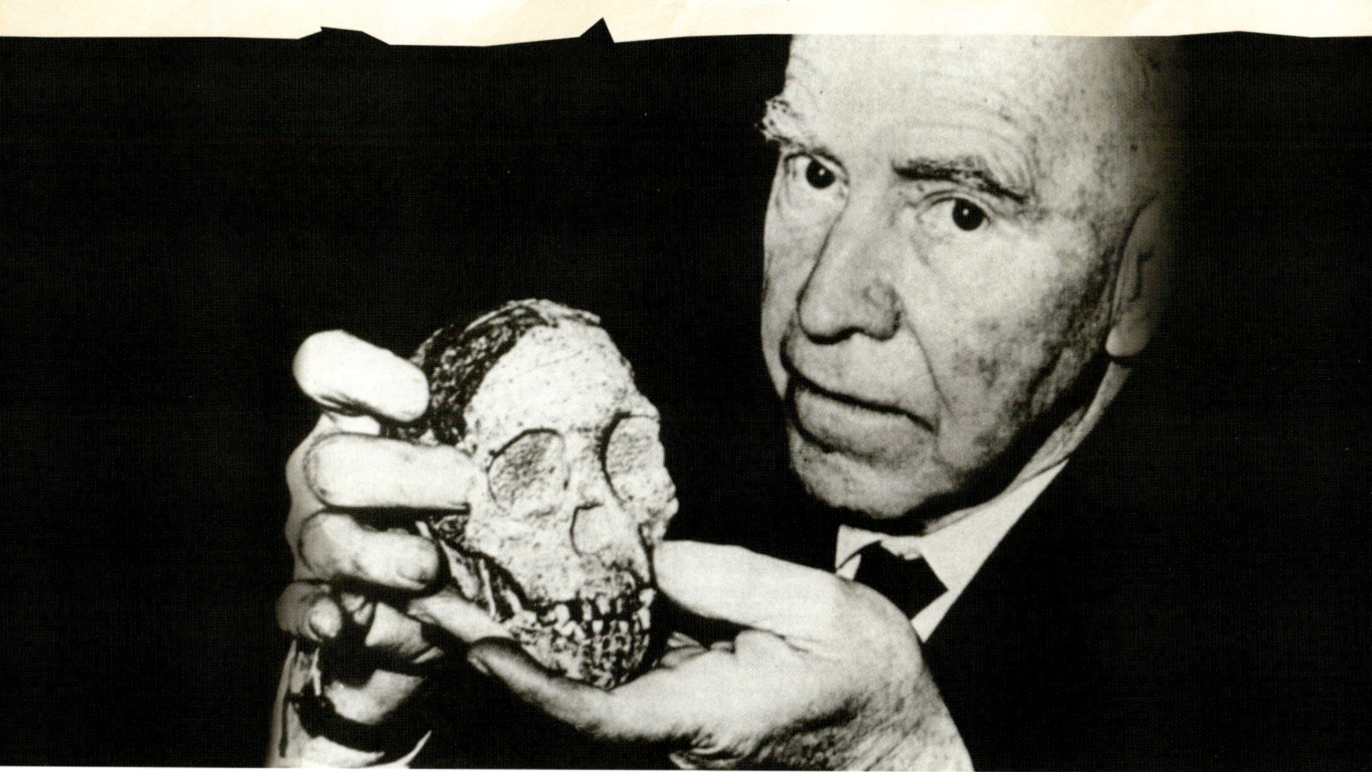

identified an adult skull of the same species as Taung Child in South Africa. After studying this find, many scientists believed Taung Child was from an ancient human ancestor species. By the 1940s, experts considered Africa the likely location of human origins.

EXCAVATING LUCY

Africa was now the center of early human excavation. Many scientists began digs there. In 1974, US archaeologist Donald C. Johanson was on a dig in Hadar, Ethiopia. Johanson came across a bone sticking out of a hillside.

That bone was the forearm of an early human. It was one of dozens of fossils found at the site. Erosion had exposed many of these fossils. To excavate them, Johanson and his team used handheld tools such as rock hammers and picks.

The scientists found a skull bone, ribs, and more. Together, the bones made up 40 percent of a skeleton. Johanson's team nicknamed the skeleton "Lucy."

Johanson and other scientists determined Lucy had been a female adult of about 20 years old. They based these details on the condition of Lucy's teeth and the width of her **pelvis**. Further examination of Lucy's features would shake up the world of archaeology.

ARCHAEOLOGIST UNCOVERED

DONALD C. JOHANSON

Donald C. Johanson was born in Chicago, Illinois, in 1943. He studied **anthropology** at the University of Chicago. Johanson's first African excavation was in 1970. In 1974, he uncovered Lucy, an early human species.

Johanson's findings influenced worldwide beliefs about human **evolution.** Since the discovery, he has written several books on human origins. Today, Johanson is a professor at Arizona State University's School of Human Evolution and Social Change.

LUCY'S IMPACT

The structure of Lucy's bones told scientists that she had been **bipedal**. The femur was angled in a way that would have allowed Lucy to walk upright. This ability is a defining **trait** of early humans. But Lucy was not the first ancient species discovered with this trait. So why did she become so famous?

Researchers had long believed bipedalism was linked to larger brains. But Lucy's skull size suggested her brain was smaller than that of the Taung Child. And her skeleton was dated to about 3.2 million years. Lucy showed scientists that bipedalism appeared in earlier species than those with larger brains.

Lucy caused great excitement among scientists. The size of her brain changed archaeologists' understanding of the process of **evolution**. Lucy also pushed the timeline of human origins back by almost 500,000 years!

Lucy was less than 4 feet (1.2 m) tall and weighed 60 to 65 pounds (27 to 29 kg). Museums often display models of what Lucy might have looked like when she was alive.

This new timeline was met with little **controversy**. By this time, archaeologists had access to better tools for dating fossils. One of these tools was called radiometric dating.

Radiometric dating was a common practice by the 1950s. Scientists learned that all Earth's rocks and minerals contain **radioactive** elements. These elements break down at constant rates over time. This knowledge allows scientists to date rocks by measuring the amount of radioactive elements in them. Radiometric dating gives a more precise age for rocks and for human remains buried within them.

Johanson and his team continued to dig in Hadar into 1975. They shoveled tons of sediment from the hillsides and sifted it through sieves. They found about 200 teeth and bone pieces this way.

The team determined these fossils came from 13 individuals. The individuals were

DIG THIS!

In 2006, archaeologists found a fossilized child's skeleton near the Lucy site. They determined the child lived about 100,000 years earlier than Lucy. The skeleton was nicknamed "Lucy's Baby" because it belonged to the same species as Lucy.

nicknamed the "First Family." All were from the same species as Lucy. They were the first evidence that ancient human-like species lived in groups!

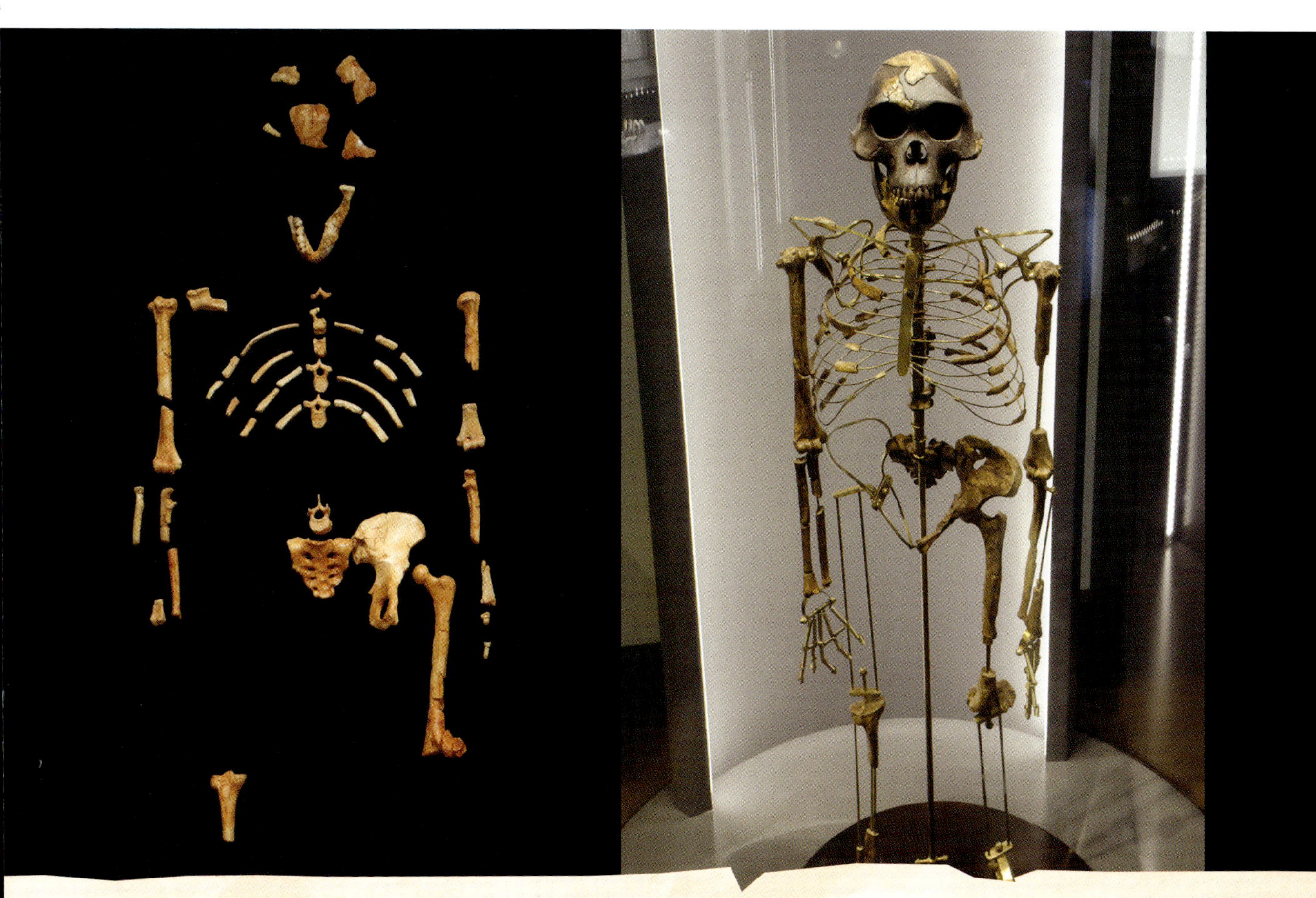

At the time of Lucy's discovery, her skeleton was the oldest and most complete early human remains ever found.

ARDI

Lucy not only changed what archaeologists thought about human **evolution**. Her discovery also made Ethiopia a key location in the search for human origins. In 1994, fossils dug up just 46 miles (74 km) from Lucy's site revealed more answers.

In November of that year, a team was excavating a site near the Awash River in Ethiopia. Student Yohannes Haile-Selassie saw something sticking up from the earth. It was two bone pieces from an early human's hand. The team dug for more.

The team eventually uncovered more than 100 bone pieces. Years later, researchers determined the bones belonged to a member of a previously unknown species. The skeleton was nicknamed "Ardi."

Ardi was dated to 4.4 million years old. This pushed the timeline of human origins back another million years! At the time, archaeologists believed the common ancestor between apes and humans lived about 5 million years ago. Ardi was very close to this missing link!

ARDI'S SKELETON

Ardi's skeleton gave researchers an idea of how Ardi likely moved around. Scientists could also determine Ardi's height and weight.

Wrists and finger joints suggest she walked on both hands and feet when in trees

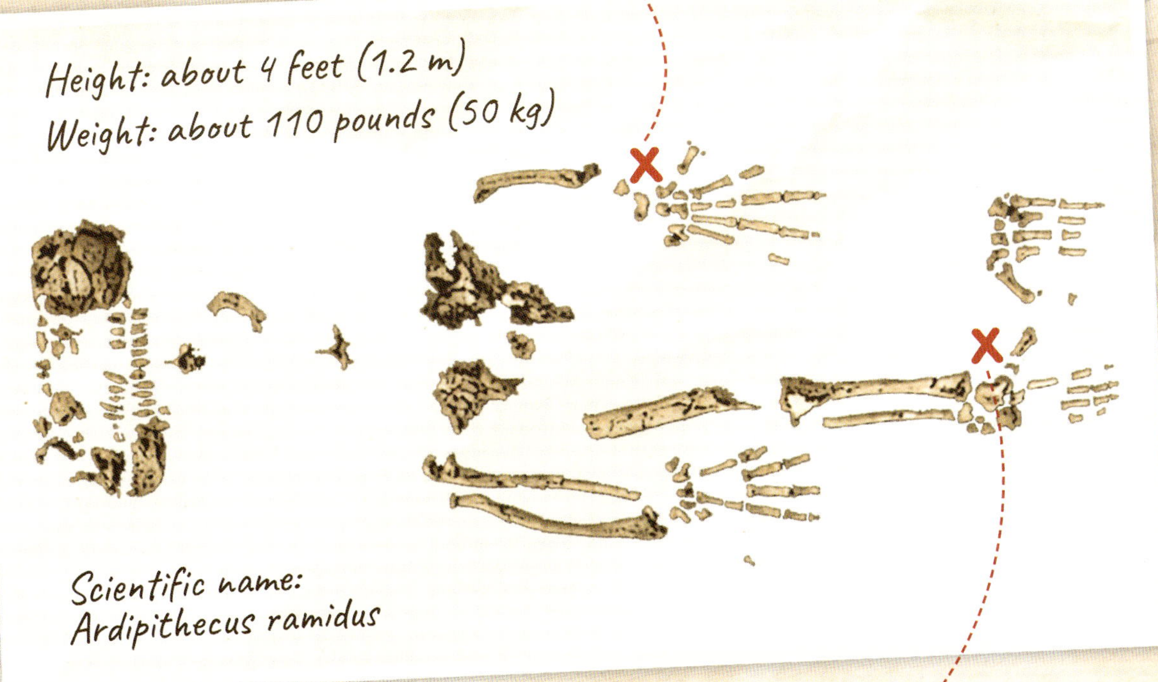

Structure of big toe suggests she could grasp tree limbs with her feet

MISSING LINK FOUND?

Several years after Ardi's discovery, an even older species was found. In 2001, French scientist Michel Brunet led a team of archaeologists on a dig in northern Chad. There, the team found an ancient skull.

The skull was ape-like in size. But the structure of its face and teeth were human-like. Brunet and his team were certain the fossil was from an early human. This was because of the placement of the spinal cord opening in the skull. It indicated the species was **bipedal**.

Brunet and his team also determined the skull was between 6 and 7 million years old. This made the split between apes and humans much earlier than previously thought. But this claim created **controversy**.

Many archaeologists agreed the fossil, nicknamed "Toumai," was likely the missing link. But some thought that it was the skull of an ancient ape. These critics argued the skull's structure would

Toumai's scientific name is *Sahelanthropus tchadensis*. The image below shows Toumai's skull from three different angles.

have prevented the species from walking upright. Other scientists believed several ancient human-like species could have lived 6 to 7 million years ago. They thought Toumai may be one of several missing link species.

TOOLS & METHODS

Toumai's claim to world's oldest human remains is **controversial**. But this isn't only because of its **anatomy**. It is also because the fossil's age could not be precisely determined. The rock layers in which Toumai was found were not suited to radiometric dating. So, researchers estimated Toumai's age based on the age of nearby fossils.

Scientists are working to create more precise dating methods. Meanwhile, today's archaeologists have advanced tools for studying finds. These include **lasers** that scan fossils and make digital casts. Computers can **analyze** these casts in ways people cannot. Scientists can quickly collect and compare fossil data from around the world.

Scientists also use special computer programs to create

DIG THIS!

Digital casts allow scientists to study a fossil without damaging it. **3-D** printers allow this too. These machines can create exact copies of fossils for further study.

In 2017, US scientist Carol Ward studied 3-million-year-old human remains without even touching them. Instead, she analyzed digital scans and 3-D prints of the fossils.

digital images of ancient human-like species. These programs can build an entire being by scanning a single human-like fossil. The programs use what scientists know about **anatomy** to imagine what a species may have looked like.

Some modern archaeologists don't need fossils to unlock secrets of human origins. Animals, including humans, leave behind traces of **DNA**. This genetic material clings to rock even after an animal's remains break down.

Scientist Viviane Slon began excavating sites for DNA in the 2010s. Slon and other researchers gathered sediment from seven locations in Europe and Asia. The team used special microscopes and other tools to examine the sediment for DNA.

In 2017, the scientists were successful. From four sites, they found nine sets of DNA. After studying the DNA, scientists determined it was from Neanderthals and an ancient human species. But how did Slon know this DNA did not come from herself or other scientists at the sites? The team knew how to spot damage that occurs to DNA over thousands of years of decay.

DNA testing could transform the process of exploring early human remains. Fossils may no longer be needed to figure out the missing links to human origins. The rock layers beneath us may hold millions of microscopic clues just waiting to be discovered!

Neanderthals are humans' closest extinct relatives. Studies have shown that many humans today carry a small percentage of Neanderthal DNA!

GLOSSARY

analyze — to determine the meaning of something by breaking down its parts.

anatomy — the branch of science that deals with the structure of animals or plants and the relationship of their parts.

anthropology — the study of the beginnings, development, and behaviors of humans and their ancestors.

bipedal — relating to a biped. A biped is an animal that walks on two legs. Bipedalism is the condition of being bipedal.

controversy — a discussion marked by strongly different views. Something that causes controversy is controversial.

DNA — a material in the body that helps determine what features a living thing will inherit. "DNA" stands for *deoxyribonucleic acid*.

embed — to enclose or set within.

environment — all the surroundings that affect the growth and well-being of a living thing.

evolve — to develop gradually. Evolution is the process of gradual development.

laser — a device that creates a narrow beam of light.

pelvis — the wide, curved bone structure between the legs and spine of a skeleton.

quarry — a place where stone is cut or blasted out for use in building.

radioactive — of, caused by, or showing radioactivity. Radioactivity is the giving off of rays of energy or particles by the breaking apart of atoms of certain elements.

3-D — having length, width, and height. "3-D" stands for *three-dimensional*.

trait — a quality or feature of something.

ONLINE RESOURCES

To learn more about early human remains, visit **abdobooklinks.com**. These links are routinely monitored and updated to provide the most current information available.

INDEX